THINK CLEAR

Simple Practices to Eliminate Overthinking

Dr. Veronica Mason

DNP-FNP-PMHNP-BC

Table of Contents

Understanding Overthinking

Causes and Impacts

Welcome to "Think Clear: Simple Practices to Eliminate Overthinking." This book is designed to help you identify, understand, and effectively manage the pervasive habit of overthinking, which can clutter your mind and disrupt your life. The journey towards mental clarity is not just about reducing thoughts; it's about nurturing healthier thinking patterns that empower you to live a more focused and fulfilling life.

The Nature of Overthinking

Overthinking is characterized by excessive and repetitive thoughts about a variety of topics, including past conversations, future possibilities, current concerns, or nothing specific at all. While thinking is a natural and necessary part of problem-solving and reflection, overthinking is when these thoughts become intrusive, preventing action and sapping motivation.

Causes of Overthinking

There are numerous triggers for overthinking. For some, it stems from anxiety or depression, turning their fears and worries into a relentless stream of thoughts. For others, it might be a byproduct of personality traits such as perfectionism, where the desire for flawless results leads to endless reviews and hesitation. Environmental factors, such as stress from work, relationships, or uncertainty about the future, also contribute significantly to overthinking.

Impacts of Overthinking

The impact of overthinking extends beyond mental discomfort. Physically, it can lead to exhaustion, insomnia, and tension headaches, as the body remains perpetually in a state of heightened stress. Emotionally, it can erode self-esteem and increase anxiety, leading to a vicious cycle where overthinking generates more stress, which in turn leads to more overthinking.

Socially, overthinkers might withdraw from relationships or activities due to fears or indecisiveness, missing out on life's experiences and opportunities for growth. Professionally, it can hinder decision-making, creativity, and productivity, as one gets caught up in the paralysis of analysis.

Purpose of This Book

This book aims to break the cycle of overthinking by providing practical, actionable strategies that you can apply to your daily life. Through a series of exercises, real-life examples, and straightforward advice, you will learn how to calm your mind, focus your thoughts, and make decisions with confidence. We will explore various techniques from mindfulness to cognitive restructuring and beyond, equipping you with a toolbox designed to tackle overthinking from multiple angles.

As you embark on this journey, remember that the goal is not to eliminate all thought, but to clear away the unnecessary noise that distracts from your values and objectives. By understanding the causes and impacts of overthinking, you are already taking the first, crucial step towards a clearer, more serene mind. Let's begin this transformative path together, learning to think clearly and live deliberately.

Chapter 1

Laying the Foundation

Welcome to the first chapter of "Think Clear: Simple Practices to Eliminate Overthinking." This chapter sets the groundwork for understanding the mechanisms behind overthinking and identifying the patterns that may be dominating your thought processes. By recognizing these patterns, you can begin to address overthinking effectively.

The Psychology of Overthinking

Overthinking often arises from our brain's natural inclination to ensure we are prepared for any threat or opportunity. This survival mechanism can, however, go awry, leading us to ruminate on problems and scenarios beyond their practical relevance. It's crucial to comprehend that overthinking is rooted in the brain's protective strategies—understanding this can make it less daunting and more manageable.

Cognitive Biases and Overthinking

- **Negativity Bias:** The brain's tendency to prioritize negative thoughts over positive ones.

- **Confirmation Bias:** Seeking information that confirms our preexisting beliefs or fears.

- **Control Illusion:** Believing we can predict and control all outcomes if we just think hard enough.

Understanding these biases helps in recognizing that overthinking is often an automatic response rather than a rational one.

Recognizing Overthinking Patterns

To start managing overthinking, it's important to first identify when and how it occurs. This section provides tools and insights to help you recognize your specific patterns of overthinking.

Common Triggers

- **Stressful Situations:** High pressure environments can trigger overthinking as you strive to find perfect solutions.

- **Decisions:** Big or small, decisions can often lead to excessive deliberation.

- **Personal Relationships:** Worrying about the stability, perceptions, or dynamics of relationships.

Signs You're Overthinking

- **Difficulty Sleeping:** Lying awake mulling over things.

- **Inability to Enjoy the Moment:** Preoccupied with 'what ifs' and 'should haves.'

- **Chronic Worry:** Constantly imagining worst-case scenarios.

Self-Assessment Tools

Engaging with self-assessment tools can provide clarity on your overthinking habits. This section includes several methods:

- **Thought Logs:** Keep a daily log of your thoughts to identify patterns and triggers.

- **Mood Tracking:** Use apps or journals to track your mood changes in relation to your thoughts.

- **Behavioral Experiments:** Test the accuracy of your negative predictions to challenge overthinking.

Setting Goals for Change

Once you've recognized your overthinking patterns, setting clear, achievable goals is essential. This isn't about eliminating all deep thinking; rather, it's about reducing unnecessary and unproductive thoughts.

- **Specificity:** Define what 'less overthinking' looks like for you. Is it less time spent ruminating? Fewer sleepless nights?

- **Measurability:** Determine how you will measure success, perhaps by reduced anxiety or improved decision-making speed.

- **Attainability:** Set realistic expectations about what can be achieved through this book's practices.

By laying this foundation, you'll be better prepared to apply the specific techniques and strategies discussed in the coming chapters to reduce overthinking effectively. This groundwork is crucial for building a stable platform from which you can start to reclaim your mental clarity and focus. Let's move forward together with a clearer understanding and practical tools to manage your thoughts more

Chapter 2

Mindfulness and Awareness

In Chapter 2 of "Think Clear: Simple Practices to Eliminate Overthinking," we explore the transformative practice of mindfulness and the role of awareness in managing your thoughts. Mindfulness is a state of active, open attention on the present. When you're mindful, you observe your thoughts and feelings from a distance, without judging them good or bad. This chapter provides practical steps to integrate mindfulness into your daily life, helping you to quiet the noise and focus more clearly.

Introduction to Mindfulness

Mindfulness involves being fully present in the moment, aware of where we are and what we're doing, and not overly reactive or overwhelmed by what's going on around us. Here's why it's particularly effective against overthinking:

- **Reduces Reactivity:** By observing your thoughts as they arise, you learn not to react automatically to them, which is crucial in breaking the cycle of overthinking.

- **Enhances Emotional Regulation:** Mindfulness helps you

understand your emotions, reducing the likelihood of spiraling into negative thought patterns.

- **Improves Focus:** Regular mindfulness practice enhances your ability to concentrate on the task at hand, rather than getting lost in your thoughts.

Daily Mindfulness Exercises

Implementing mindfulness doesn't need to be complicated. Here are several exercises designed to fit into everyday life:

- **Mindful Breathing:** This involves focusing your attention on your breath, the inhale and exhale. You can do this for a few minutes each day to help center your thoughts.

- **Sensory Observation:** Choose one sense to focus on for five minutes. For example, listen to the sounds in your environment without labeling or judging them.

- **Mindful Eating:** Eat slowly and without distraction, focusing on the taste, texture, and sensations of your food.

The Role of Awareness in Controlling Thoughts

Building on mindfulness, developing a heightened sense of awareness about your thought processes is essential. Awareness allows you to recognize the onset of overthinking and decide how to deal with it:

- **Identify Thought Patterns:** Notice when your thoughts begin to loop or spiral. Label these patterns as they occur.

- **Set Intentional Breaks:** When you catch yourself overthinking, give yourself permission to step back. This might mean setting aside specific times when you allow yourself to reflect or worry.

- **Use 'Thought Stopping' Techniques:** Say "stop" out loud when you recognize an unhelpful thought pattern. This can interrupt the flow of repetitive thoughts.

Integrating Mindfulness into Daily Routines

To make mindfulness a part of your life, integrate it into your daily routines:

- **Morning Routine:** Start your day with a five-minute mindfulness meditation. This sets a calm, clear tone for the day ahead.

- **Workday Integration:** Before starting a new task, take a moment to center yourself with a few deep breaths.

- **Evening Wind-Down:** Reflect on the day with a gratitude exercise, noting three things you were thankful for, to focus on positive experiences rather than worries.

Challenges and Tips for Consistent Practice

Practicing mindfulness can be challenging, especially when dealing with persistent overthinking. Here are some tips to maintain consistency:

- **Routine:** Incorporate mindfulness at the same times each day to build a habit.

- **Patience:** Be patient with yourself. Mindfulness is a skill that takes time to develop.

- **Community:** Engage with a community or group that practices mindfulness. This can provide support and motivation.

By embracing mindfulness and awareness, you equip yourself with powerful tools to manage overthinking. These practices foster a state of mental clarity where thoughts serve you rather than control you. As we proceed to the next chapters, we'll build on these foundations, adding more strategies to your toolkit for managing overthinking.

Cognitive Restructuring Techniques

In Chapter 3 of "Think Clear: Simple Practices to Eliminate Overthinking," we delve into cognitive restructuring, a powerful psychological tool used to challenge and change unhelpful thought patterns. This technique is essential for those who frequently find themselves trapped in cycles of overthinking, as it helps reframe negative thoughts into more positive, realistic ones.

Identifying and Challenging Distorted Thoughts

Cognitive distortions are irrational thought patterns that reinforce negative thinking and emotions. Recognizing these patterns is the first step in cognitive restructuring.

Common Cognitive Distortions:

- **All-or-Nothing Thinking:** Seeing things in black and white categories.

- **Overgeneralization:** Viewing a single negative event as a never-ending pattern of defeat.

- **Mental Filtering:** Only paying attention to certain types of evidence.

- **Jumping to Conclusions:** Interpreting things negatively without any definitive facts.

To challenge these distortions, you need to first identify them through thought recording. Once identified, question their validity and explore more balanced perspectives.

Steps to Challenge Distorted Thoughts:

1. **Identify the Thought:** Write down the automatic negative thought.

2. **Assess the Evidence:** Consider the evidence both for and against the thought.

3. **Consider Alternatives:** Are there other ways to view the situation?

4. **Use a Balanced Statement:** Replace the distorted thought with a more accurate and balanced one.

Building Rational Thinking Habits

Developing rational thinking is about creating a balanced mindset that evaluates thoughts based on facts rather than feelings.

Techniques to Foster Rational Thinking:

- **The Double-Standard Method:** Talk to yourself in the same compassionate way you would talk to a friend.

- **The Experimental Technique:** Test your beliefs against real-life experiences.

- **Cost-Benefit Analysis:** Weigh the costs and benefits of worrying or thinking negatively about a situation.

Practical Applications of Cognitive Behavioral Techniques

Cognitive Behavioral Therapy (CBT) techniques are particularly effective in managing overthinking and can be practiced independently.

Behavioral Experiments:

Conduct experiments to test the validity of your negative predictions. For example, if you believe that speaking up in meetings will result in ridicule, try contributing to a discussion and observe the outcomes.

Scheduling Worry Time:

Set aside a specific time and place for worrying. During this period, allow yourself to worry about whatever is on your mind, but once the time is up, move on to more productive activities. This confines worry to a small part of your day, making it easier to manage.

Mindfulness-Based Cognitive Therapy (MBCT):

Combine mindfulness practices with cognitive therapy to deal with distressing thoughts more effectively. Mindfulness helps you recognize the arrival of overthinking patterns, and cognitive therapy provides the tools to address them.

The Role of Journaling in Cognitive Restructuring

Keeping a thought diary not only helps in identifying recurring distorted thoughts but also in understanding the context and triggers for overthinking. Journal prompts can be specifically designed to foster cognitive restructuring:

- **Prompt:** "What evidence do I have that supports or contradicts this thought?"

- **Prompt:** "Is there a more positive, realistic way of looking at this situation?"

Conclusion

Cognitive restructuring is a vital skill for anyone looking to reduce overthinking. By learning to recognize and challenge unhelpful thought patterns, you can significantly alter the way you interpret and respond to events in your life. This chapter has equipped you with the tools needed to begin practicing these techniques. As we move forward, remember that consistency is key in making these cognitive changes lasting and effective. Let's continue to build on these strategies, enhancing your ability to think clearly and live more peacefully.

Stress Management and Relaxation

In Chapter 4 of "Think Clear: Simple Practices to Eliminate Overthinking," we focus on managing stress and embracing relaxation techniques. Stress is a common trigger for overthinking, causing the mind to spin into overdrive as it tries to anticipate and plan for every possible scenario. By learning effective stress management and relaxation strategies, you can reduce the intensity and frequency of overthinking episodes.

Understanding the Link Between Stress and Overthinking

Stress activates the body's "fight or flight" response, which can lead to an onslaught of rapid, often irrational thoughts. Understanding this link is crucial because it helps frame overthinking as a natural reaction to stress rather than a personal flaw.

- **Physiological Effects:** Stress can lead to increased adrenaline and cortisol, making your body and mind less able to engage in calm, rational thought.

- **Cognitive Effects:** Under stress, your ability to process information efficiently and make decisions can become impaired, often leading to overthinking.

Relaxation Techniques That Work

Integrating relaxation techniques into your daily routine can help you manage stress and reduce overthinking. Here are several effective methods:

Deep Breathing Exercises

- **Technique:** Focus on slow, deep breaths from the diaphragm to reduce the body's stress response.

- **Practice:** Try 4-7-8 breathing—inhale for 4 seconds, hold for 7 seconds, and exhale for 8 seconds.

Progressive Muscle Relaxation (PMR)

- **Technique:** Tense each muscle group for about five seconds and then relax it for 30 seconds, working your way through the body.

- **Practice:** Start from the toes and move upwards to the head.

Guided Imagery

- **Technique:** Use your imagination to visualize a peaceful, relaxing place or situation.

- **Practice:** Spend a few minutes in this 'mental retreat' when feeling overwhelmed.

Creating a Personal Stress Management Plan

A tailored stress management plan can empower you to handle stressful situations more effectively, thereby reducing the tendency to overthink.

- **Identify Stressors:** Keep a journal to identify which situations trigger stress and overthinking.

- **Develop Responses:** For each stressor, list healthy ways to cope or manage these situations.

- **Implement Routine:** Incorporate regular stress-reduction techniques into your daily life to maintain a baseline of calm.

The Role of Regular Exercise

Physical activity is a powerful stress reliever. It not only uses up excess energy released by the fight or flight response but also helps elevate mood by releasing endorphins.

- **Types of Exercise:** Aerobic activities like walking, running, and cycling are particularly effective.

- **Routine:** Aim for at least 30 minutes of moderate exercise most days of the week.

Mindfulness Meditation

Mindfulness meditation teaches you to focus on the present moment, which can be especially helpful in managing stress-related overthinking.

- **Practice:** Regular mindfulness practice can help you recognize when you're starting to overthink and allow you to redirect your attention back to the present.

- **Benefits:** Over time, this practice can decrease the overall level of stress and anxiety.

Sleep Hygiene

Poor sleep can exacerbate stress and overthinking. Establishing a healthy sleep routine can significantly improve your ability to manage both.

- **Strategies:** Create a calming bedtime routine, keep a consistent sleep schedule, and optimize your bedroom environment for sleep.

- **Benefits:** Better sleep can lead to improved mood, enhanced brain function, and reduced stress levels.

Conclusion

Effective stress management and relaxation techniques are essential tools for anyone looking to reduce overthinking. By understanding and mitigating the impact of stress on your mind and body, you can enhance your overall well-being and mental clarity. As you continue to apply these strategies, remember that consistency is key to long-term success. Let's proceed with the skills and knowledge to embrace a more relaxed and focused life

Lifestyle Adjustments

Chapter 5 of "Think Clear: Simple Practices to Eliminate Overthinking" explores the critical role of lifestyle adjustments in managing and reducing overthinking. By making conscious changes to your daily habits, you can significantly influence your mental health and cognitive patterns. This chapter provides practical advice on how diet, exercise, sleep, and environmental changes can help you achieve a clearer mind.

The Influence of Diet on Mental Health

What you eat directly affects the structure and function of your brain and, ultimately, your mood and thought processes.

Balanced Diet Benefits

- **Boost Brain Function:** Foods rich in omega-3 fatty acids, antioxidants, and vitamins support brain health and can improve cognitive function.

- **Stabilize Mood:** A diet that stabilizes blood sugar with whole grains and minimizes caffeine and sugar can help reduce mood swings and anxiety.

Recommended Foods

- **Fatty Fish:** Salmon, trout, and sardines for omega-3 fatty acids.

- **Nuts and Seeds:** Walnuts, flaxseeds, and chia seeds for healthy fats.

- **Leafy Greens:** Spinach and kale for vitamins and minerals.

- **Whole Grains:** Oats, quinoa, and whole wheat to maintain blood sugar levels.

Regular Physical Activity

Exercise is not only crucial for your physical health but also your mental health, helping to manage stress and reduce overthinking.

Exercise Benefits

- **Reduces Stress:** Physical activity helps reduce fatigue, improves alertness and concentration, and enhances overall cognitive function.

- **Enhances Endorphins:** Exercise produces endorphins (the body's feel-good neurotransmitters), which act as natural painkillers and mood elevators.

Activity Suggestions

- **Aerobic Exercises:** Such as swimming, cycling, and running.

- **Strength Training:** Focus on major muscle groups a few times a week.

- **Yoga and Tai Chi:** Combine physical movement with meditation to improve mental and physical health.

Importance of Sleep in Thought Regulation

Sleep plays a pivotal role in thinking and learning. Lack of sleep affects both your mental and physical health.

Sleep Hygiene Tips

- **Consistency:** Go to bed and wake up at the same time every day.

- **Environment:** Ensure your bedroom is conducive to sleep—quiet, dark, and cool.

- **Pre-sleep Routine:** Develop a calming bedtime routine that may include reading, light stretching, or meditation.

Optimizing Your Environment

The spaces where you spend your time can significantly influence your mental state and susceptibility to overthinking.

Environmental Adjustments

- **Clutter-Free Spaces:** Reduce clutter to minimize cognitive overload and distraction.

- **Nature and Light:** Increase exposure to natural light and green spaces to boost mood and focus.

- **Personal Comfort:** Adjust temperature, lighting, and ergonomics to optimize comfort and productivity.

Mindful Technology Use

Technology can be a significant source of stress and distraction, contributing to overthinking.

Managing Technology

- **Set Boundaries:** Designate specific times to check emails and social media.

- **Digital Detox:** Consider regular intervals where you disconnect from digital devices to clear your mind.

- **Mindful Consumption:** Be selective about the content you consume, focusing on positivity and education over sensationalism and drama.

Conclusion

Lifestyle adjustments are a powerful tool in the fight against overthinking. By taking control of your diet, exercise, sleep, and environment, you can foster a mental landscape that is more conducive to peace and productivity. As we continue into the next chapters, remember that each small change you implement can have a profound impact on your overall mental clarity and quality of life. Let's move forward with the knowledge and strategies to make these beneficial lifestyle shifts.

Chapter 6

Setting Goals and Priorities

In Chapter 6 of "Think Clear: Simple Practices to Eliminate Overthinking," we focus on the essential skills of setting goals and prioritizing tasks, which can significantly reduce overthinking by clarifying what matters most. Effective goal-setting and prioritization help streamline decision-making processes and alleviate the stress that often triggers excessive thinking.

Understanding the Importance of Clear Goals

Setting clear, achievable goals is fundamental to reducing overthinking. Goals provide direction and a benchmark for measuring progress, both of which are crucial for maintaining focus and minimizing unnecessary deliberation.

- **Direction and Focus:** Clear goals help direct your mental energy towards productive activities instead of getting lost in endless cycles of what-ifs.

- **Sense of Control:** Well-defined goals can increase your sense of control over your life, which reduces anxiety and the tendency to overthink.

How to Set Realistic Goals

Realistic goals are achievable and aligned with your abilities and commitments. Here's how to set goals that are both challenging and attainable:

Specificity

- **Define Clear Outcomes:** Avoid vague goals like "do better." Instead, opt for specific targets, such as "increase monthly sales by 10%."

Measurability

- **Quantify Your Goals:** Ensure that your goals can be measured, so you know when they have been achieved. For instance, instead of "write more," set a goal to "write 500 words per day."

Achievability

- **Assess Resources and Constraints:** Consider what resources you have and what limitations you might face to ensure your goals are within reach.

Relevance

- **Align Goals With Values:** Your goals should reflect your values and larger life plans to ensure they are meaningful and motivating.

Time-Bound

- **Set Deadlines:** Having a deadline helps keep you focused and working toward completion.

Prioritizing Tasks to Reduce Anxiety and Overthinking

Once goals are set, prioritizing tasks is the next step. It helps manage time and resources efficiently, reducing the burden of feeling like everything needs immediate attention.

Eisenhower Box

- **Urgent vs. Important:** Use this tool to divide tasks into four categories: urgent and important, important but not urgent, urgent but not important, and neither urgent nor important.

The Pareto Principle (80/20 Rule)

- **Focus on High-Impact Activities:** Identify the 20% of activities that will yield 80% of results, and prioritize these tasks.

The Power of Saying 'No'

Learning to say 'no' is crucial for managing your workload and reducing overthinking.

- **Protect Your Time:** Be selective about taking on new commitments. Saying no to less critical tasks gives you the time to focus on achieving your goals.

- **Reduce Overload:** Overcommitment can lead to stress and trigger overthinking. Prioritize your mental health and well-being by keeping your workload manageable.

Techniques for Effective Time Management

Effective time management is vital for reducing stress and overthinking. Here are some techniques to help manage your time better:

- **Time Blocking:** Allocate specific blocks of time for different activities. This helps reduce the anxiety of when and how tasks will be completed.

- **Pomodoro Technique:** Work in short sprints of 25 minutes followed by a 5-minute break to maintain focus and clarity.

Conclusion

Setting goals and priorities is more than a productivity technique; it's a fundamental skill for mental clarity and reducing overthinking. By knowing what needs to be done and when you can clear your mind of unnecessary clutter and focus on what truly matters. As you implement these strategies, you will find yourself more capable of navigating life's challenges with a calm and decisive mindset. Let's carry these skills into our daily lives and continue building a foundation for a clearer, more focused existence.

Chapter 7

Embracing Imperfection

In Chapter 7 of "Think Clear: Simple Practices to Eliminate Overthinking," we explore the concept of embracing imperfection, a crucial step in reducing the pressure that fuels overthinking. Perfectionism can often be a significant driver of excessive thinking, as the quest for flawless outcomes can lead to endless cycles of rumination and self-doubt. This chapter discusses strategies for accepting imperfection in various aspects of life, which can liberate your mind and enhance overall well-being.

Understanding Perfectionism and Its Dangers

Perfectionism isn't just about striving for excellence; it involves setting unrealistically high standards and valuing yourself based on your ability to meet these standards. This mindset can lead to:

- **Fear of Failure:** Avoiding new challenges due to the fear of not meeting high standards.

- **Procrastination:** Delaying tasks because you feel you can't perform them perfectly.

- **Chronic Stress:** Experiencing continuous stress due to the

28

relentless pursuit of perfection.

Techniques to Accept Imperfection

Adopting a more flexible approach to your goals and tasks can significantly reduce stress and mitigate overthinking. Here are some techniques to help you embrace imperfection:

Set Realistic Standards

- **Review Expectations:** Regularly assess and adjust your standards to ensure they are realistic and attainable.

- **Celebrate Small Wins:** Recognize and celebrate achievements that may not be perfect but represent significant progress.

Cognitive Restructuring

- **Challenge Perfectionist Thoughts:** Use cognitive restructuring techniques (discussed in Chapter 3) to challenge and modify perfectionist thinking patterns.

- **Reframe Mistakes as Learning Opportunities:** View failures as essential parts of the learning process, not as reflections of your worth.

Mindfulness and Self-Compassion

- **Practice Mindfulness:** Stay present and reduce judgment by observing your thoughts and feelings without labeling them as good or bad.

- **Cultivate Self-Compassion:** Be kind to yourself when things don't go as planned. Use comforting words and acknowledge that everyone makes mistakes.

Building Flexibility into Daily Life

Incorporating flexibility in how you approach tasks and goals can reduce the pressure to perform perfectly.

- **Flexible Scheduling:** Allow for adjustments in your schedule and task list to accommodate the unexpected.

- **Prioritize Effort Over Outcome:** Focus on the effort you put into tasks, rather than obsessing over the perfect outcome.

Letting Go of Control

Learning to let go of the need to control every detail of every situation can significantly decrease overthinking.

- **Delegate Tasks:** Trust others with responsibilities to help alleviate the burden of needing to handle everything yourself.

- **Accept Uncertainty:** Recognize that not all aspects of life are controllable, and embrace the unknown as an opportunity for growth.

Conclusion

Embracing imperfection is about shifting your perspective from a focus on flawless execution to a more balanced appreciation of effort and progress. By accepting that imperfection is a natural part of being human, you can reduce the mental load of overthinking and lead a more fulfilling life. As we continue to explore these concepts, remember that the journey toward reducing overthinking is not about achieving perfection in your methods, but about finding peace and functionality in the imperfection of everyday life. Let's carry these lessons forward, cultivating resilience and flexibility as we navigate our complex world.

Building Resilience

Chapter 8 of "Think Clear: Simple Practices to Eliminate Overthinking" is devoted to building resilience—the ability to bounce back from setbacks, adapt to change, and keep going in the face of adversity. Resilience is a crucial skill for reducing overthinking, as it helps you handle stress more effectively and maintain a clear mind even under pressure. This chapter explores strategies to strengthen your mental and emotional resilience, providing a foundation for a more robust response to life's challenges.

Understanding Resilience

Resilience is not about avoiding stress or difficulties; rather, it's about your ability to cope with and rise above challenges. Resilient individuals are better equipped to manage their thoughts during stressful times, preventing these situations from leading to excessive overthinking.

- **Components of Resilience:** Awareness, flexibility, perseverance, and the ability to utilize support systems effectively.

Tools for Building Mental and Emotional Resilience

Develop a Growth Mindset

- **Embrace Challenges:** View challenges as opportunities to grow rather than obstacles to fear.

- **Learn from Mistakes:** See mistakes as part of the learning process, not as permanent setbacks.

Strengthen Problem-Solving Skills

- **Break Problems Down:** Tackle challenges by breaking them into manageable parts.

- **Seek Multiple Solutions:** Encourage creative thinking by looking for various solutions to a problem.

Enhance Emotional Regulation

- **Mindfulness Practices:** Engage regularly in practices that enhance emotional awareness and control, such as meditation and breathing exercises.

- **Emotional Awareness:** Cultivate an understanding of your emotional triggers and how they influence your thoughts.

Overcoming Setbacks with a Clear Mind

Learning to deal with setbacks efficiently is essential for maintaining mental clarity and preventing overthinking.

- **Reframe Your Perspective:** Shift how you perceive setbacks by framing them as temporary and surmountable.

- **Stay Focused on Your Goals:** Keep your long-term goals in perspective, which can help maintain motivation even in difficult times.

Stories of Resilience and Recovery

Incorporating narratives of people who have overcome significant challenges can be incredibly inspiring. These stories not only provide practical examples of resilience but also help normalize the struggles involved in the process.

- **Case Studies:** Detailed accounts of how individuals have managed and recovered from failure.

- **Lessons Learned:** Key takeaways from each story that readers can apply in their own lives.

Building a Support Network

A robust support network is vital for resilience. Knowing you have people to turn to can lessen the burden of difficult times.

- **Seek Supportive Relationships:** Foster relationships with people who offer encouragement and understand your challenges.

- **Professional Help:** Recognize when it's time to seek professional advice or counseling to help manage overwhelming thoughts.

Maintaining Resilience Long-Term

Building and maintaining resilience is an ongoing process. Continuous effort and commitment to personal growth are necessary to sustain the benefits.

- **Regular Self-Reflection:** Periodically assess your resilience strategies and make adjustments as needed.

- **Lifelong Learning:** Commit to continuous learning and self-improvement to adapt to new challenges effectively.

Conclusion

Building resilience is a powerful defense against overthinking. By enhancing your ability to cope with stress, adapt to change, and recover from setbacks, you equip yourself with the tools necessary to maintain clarity of thought and purpose. As we move forward, remember that resilience is not an innate quality but a skill that can be developed and strengthened over time. Embrace these strategies to build a resilient mind, ready to face whatever challenges life may bring.

Advanced Practices for Persistent Overthinkers

In Chapter 9 of "Think Clear: Simple Practices to Eliminate Overthinking," we address the needs of those who find that standard mindfulness and cognitive restructuring techniques are not fully managing their overthinking tendencies. This chapter is designed for individuals who experience persistent overthinking and seek more intensive strategies to achieve mental clarity. Here, we delve into advanced practices that offer deeper insight and more robust tools for those needing additional support.

When to Seek Professional Help

Recognizing when you need professional assistance is crucial in managing severe overthinking effectively. This section helps you identify the signs that indicate a need for professional intervention.

- **Persistent Distress:** When overthinking is constant and significantly impacts your daily life, professional help may be necessary.

- **Impact on Functioning:** If your ability to work, maintain relationships, or perform daily activities is impaired, it's time to seek help.

- **Ineffectiveness of Basic Techniques:** When standard techniques don't bring relief, a mental health professional can provide specialized therapies.

Integrating Advanced Mindfulness and Meditation Techniques

While basic mindfulness practices are beneficial, more advanced techniques can offer deeper levels of insight and relief for persistent overthinkers.

Mindfulness-Based Stress Reduction (MBSR)

- **Structured Program:** This structured 8-week program includes mindfulness training to help people better handle stress and anxiety.

- **Techniques Included:** Body scanning, meditation, and simple yoga poses.

Mindfulness-Based Cognitive Therapy (MBCT)

- **Purpose:** MBCT combines mindfulness practices with cognitive therapy to prevent the recurrence of depression, particularly useful for overthinkers with depressive tendencies.

Long-term Strategies for Maintaining Mental Clarity

Maintaining mental clarity over the long term requires ongoing commitment and adaptation of strategies to meet evolving needs.

Routine Reassessment

- **Review and Adjust:** Regularly assess the effectiveness of your practices and make necessary adjustments.

- **Stay Informed:** Keep up with the latest research and developments in psychological health to enhance your practices.

Sustained Learning and Growth

- **Continuous Education:** Engage in workshops, courses, and reading to deepen your understanding of mental health and resilience.

- **Peer Support Groups:** Consider joining groups where you can share experiences and strategies with others facing similar challenges.

Holistic Health Approaches

Addressing overthinking might also involve looking at holistic health practices that align the body and mind.

Integrative Nutrition

- **Diet and Mental Health:** Explore the impact of nutrition on mental health with a focus on foods that reduce inflammation and support cognitive function.

Physical Wellness

- **Exercise as Therapy:** Advanced exercise routines that not only improve physical health but also enhance mental clarity, like high-intensity interval training (HIIT) or martial arts.

Conclusion

For those dealing with persistent overthinking, advancing beyond basic practices can be necessary. This chapter aims to provide you with a deeper understanding and more comprehensive tools to manage your thoughts effectively. Embracing a combination of professional help, advanced mindfulness techniques, and holistic approaches can lead to significant improvements in your mental clarity and overall well-being. As we close this book, remember that the journey to clear thinking is continuous and often requires adapting and expanding your strategies to meet your changing needs.

Conclusion

As we conclude "Think Clear: Simple Practices to Eliminate Overthinking," it's important to reflect on the journey we've embarked upon together. This book has been designed as a guide to help you navigate the challenges of overthinking, providing you with a toolbox of strategies aimed at fostering mental clarity and reducing the noise of excessive thoughts.

Recap of Key Strategies

Throughout the chapters, we've explored a variety of practices, each tailored to address specific aspects of overthinking:

- **Understanding Overthinking:** We began by identifying the roots and impacts of overthinking, setting the stage for why it's crucial to address this habit.

- **Mindfulness and Awareness:** Learning to anchor yourself in the present moment reduces the tendency to dwell on past errors or future worries.

- **Cognitive Restructuring:** Techniques to challenge and change the negative thought patterns that fuel overthinking.

- **Stress Management:** Effective ways to manage stress that can trigger or worsen overthinking.

- **Lifestyle Adjustments:** Modifications in your daily life that can enhance your mental health and reduce the likelihood of overthinking.

- **Setting Goals and Priorities:** How clear objectives and organized priorities can streamline your thinking process.

- **Embracing Imperfection:** Accepting that imperfection is part of being human can significantly lower the stakes of everyday decisions and interactions.

- **Building Resilience:** Developing the ability to bounce back from setbacks, which can help maintain mental clarity under stress.

- **Advanced Practices for Persistent Overthinkers:** For those who need deeper intervention, advanced strategies and when to seek professional help.

The Path Forward

The journey to overcome overthinking is deeply personal and varies from one individual to another. While the strategies outlined in this book provide a solid foundation, true progress comes from consistent practice and personal adaptation of these methods. It's about building a toolkit that works for you, one that resonates with your personal experiences and challenges.

A Lifelong Commitment

Reducing overthinking is not a destination but a continuous process of growth and self-discovery. It requires a commitment to self-care and mental health that extends beyond the pages of this book. As you implement these practices, you will likely discover more about yourself and how your mind operates. This knowledge is powerful—it not only serves to reduce overthinking but also enhances your overall well-being.

Encouragement for the Future

Remember, every step you take is a part of your journey towards clearer thinking and a more fulfilled life. Mistakes and setbacks are not failures, but opportunities for learning and growth. Embrace them with the resilience and strategies you have learned here.

As you close this book, take with you the understanding that you are capable of controlling your thought processes and that you have the tools to lead a more thoughtful, intentional life. Keep moving forward, keep practicing, and keep believing in your ability to think clear. The path to a quieter mind is through persistent practice and the courage to face your thoughts head-on. Thank you for allowing this book to be a part of your journey to a clearer, more focused life.

Appendix A: Worksheets and Exercises

This appendix provides a collection of practical worksheets and exercises designed to help you implement the techniques discussed in "Think Clear: Simple Practices to Eliminate Overthinking." These tools are intended to enhance your understanding and facilitate the application of strategies to reduce overthinking and improve mental clarity.

1. Mindfulness Meditation Guides

Breathing Meditation Exercise

1. **Find a Quiet Space:** Choose a quiet place where you won't be disturbed.

2. **Set a Timer:** Start with 5-10 minutes and gradually increase the duration as you become more comfortable.

3. **Sit Comfortably:** Sit in a comfortable position with your back straight and hands resting on your knees.

4. **Focus on Your Breath:** Close your eyes and focus on your breath. Notice the sensation of air entering and leaving your nostrils.

5. **Return to Your Breath:** When your mind wanders, gently bring your focus back to your breath without judgment.

Body Scan Meditation Exercise

1. **Lie Down or Sit Comfortably:** Find a comfortable position, either lying down or sitting.

2. **Close Your Eyes:** Gently close your eyes and take a few deep breaths.

3. **Focus on Your Body:** Start from the top of your head and gradually move your attention down to your toes, noticing any sensations in each part of your body.

4. **Breathe Through Tension:** If you encounter areas of tension, imagine breathing into those areas and releasing the tension with each exhale.

5. **Complete the Scan:** Once you reach your toes, take a few deep breaths and slowly open your eyes.

2. Cognitive Restructuring Sheets

Identifying Negative Thoughts

- **Situation:** Describe the situation that triggered your overthinking.

- **Negative Thoughts:** List the negative thoughts that came to your mind.

- **Evidence For:** Write down the evidence that supports these thoughts.

- **Evidence Against:** Write down the evidence that contradicts these thoughts.

- **Alternative Thought:** Develop a more balanced, realistic thought.

Challenging Cognitive Distortions

- **Situation:** Describe the situation causing you distress.

- **Cognitive Distortion:** Identify the type of cognitive distortion (e.g., all-or-nothing thinking, overgeneralization).

- **Challenge the Distortion:** Ask yourself questions like:

  - Is this thought based on facts or feelings?

  - How would a friend view this situation?

  - What evidence do I have for and against this thought?

- **New Perspective:** Write down a new, balanced perspective.

3. Stress Management Plans

Developing a Personal Stress Management Plan

- **Identify Stressors:** List the main sources of stress in your life.

- **Current Coping Strategies:** Write down how you currently cope with these stressors.

- **Evaluate Effectiveness:** Assess the effectiveness of your current coping strategies.

- **New Strategies:** Identify new strategies to manage stress more effectively (e.g., exercise, time management, hobbies).

- **Action Plan:** Create a step-by-step plan to implement these new strategies in your daily routine.

Daily Stress Log

- **Date and Time:** Note the date and time of the stressful event.

- **Situation:** Describe the situation that caused stress.

- **Response:** Write down how you responded to the stress.

- **Coping Strategies:** List the coping strategies you used.

- **Effectiveness:** Rate the effectiveness of your response and coping strategies on a scale of 1 to 10.

4. Goal Setting Worksheets

SMART Goals Worksheet

- **Specific:** Clearly define your goal.

- **Measurable:** Determine how you will measure your progress.

- **Achievable:** Ensure your goal is realistic and attainable.

- **Relevant:** Make sure the goal is important to you and aligns with your values.

- **Time-Bound:** Set a deadline for achieving your goal.

Example:

- **Goal:** I want to reduce my overthinking about work.

- **Specific:** I will practice mindfulness meditation for 10 minutes each morning.

- **Measurable:** I will track my meditation sessions in a journal.

- **Achievable:** I can easily fit 10 minutes of meditation into my morning routine.

- **Relevant:** Reducing overthinking will improve my mental well-being and productivity.

- **Time-Bound:** I will practice this for the next 30 days and then evaluate my progress.

5. Journaling Prompts

Daily Reflection Prompts

- **Morning Prompt:** What are my top three priorities for today?

- **Evening Prompt:** What went well today, and why?

- **Gratitude Prompt:** What am I grateful for today?

- **Challenge Prompt:** What challenged me today, and how did I respond?

Weekly Reflection Prompts

- **Accomplishments:** What did I accomplish this week?

- **Lessons Learned:** What lessons did I learn from any challenges I faced?

- **Mindfulness:** How often did I practice mindfulness or meditation this week?

- **Goals:** What are my goals for the upcoming week?

6. Additional Exercises

Visualization Techniques

- **Guided Imagery:** Imagine yourself in a peaceful, relaxing place. Use all your senses to make the image as vivid as possible.

- **Future Visualization:** Visualize yourself successfully overcoming a current challenge. Focus on the positive emotions associated with this success.

Progressive Muscle Relaxation

1. **Find a Quiet Space:** Sit or lie down in a comfortable position.

2. **Tense Muscle Groups:** Starting with your toes, tense each muscle group for 5-10 seconds.

3. **Release Tension:** Gradually release the tension and notice the difference in sensation.

4. **Progress Up the Body:** Move progressively up your body, tensing and relaxing each muscle group.

These worksheets and exercises are designed to help you put into practice the strategies discussed in "Think Clear: Simple Practices to Eliminate Overthinking." Use them regularly to reinforce your learning and achieve greater mental clarity.

Appendix B: Journaling Prompts

Journaling can be a powerful tool for reducing overthinking by helping you process your thoughts, identify patterns, and gain clarity. This appendix provides a collection of journaling prompts designed to facilitate reflective thinking and support the techniques discussed in "Think Clear: Simple Practices to Eliminate Overthinking." Use these prompts regularly to deepen your understanding of your thought processes and cultivate a clearer mind.

1. Daily Reflection Prompts

Morning Prompts

1. **What are my top three priorities for today?**

   - Start your day with clear goals to help focus your thoughts and actions.

2. **What positive affirmations can I use to start my day?**

   - Set a positive tone for the day with affirmations that promote confidence and clarity.

3. **What is one thing I can do today to be kind to myself?**

   - Plan a small act of self-care to enhance your well-being.

4. **What might challenge me today, and how can I prepare?**

   - Anticipate potential obstacles and plan proactive strategies to handle them.

Evening Prompts

1. **What went well today, and why?**

   - Reflect on positive experiences to reinforce good habits and increase gratitude.

2. **What did I learn today?**

   - Identify new insights or lessons from your experiences.

3. **What could I have done differently?**

   - Consider alternative actions or responses to improve future outcomes.

4. **What am I grateful for today?**

   - Cultivate a habit of gratitude by acknowledging positive aspects of your day.

2. Weekly Reflection Prompts

Weekly Review Prompts

1. **What were my major accomplishments this week?**

   - Recognize and celebrate your successes to boost motivation and self-esteem.

2. **What challenges did I face, and how did I overcome them?**

   - Reflect on how you navigated difficulties to build resilience.

3. **What did I do to manage stress and overthinking?**

   - Evaluate the effectiveness of your stress management techniques.

4. **How often did I practice mindfulness or meditation this week?**

   - Assess your consistency in practicing mindfulness to identify areas for improvement.

Goal Setting Prompts

1. **What are my goals for the upcoming week?**

   - Set clear, actionable goals to maintain focus and direction.

2. **What steps will I take to achieve these goals?**

   - Outline specific actions to help achieve your weekly objectives.

3. **How will I measure my progress?**

   - Determine metrics or criteria to evaluate your success.

4. **What potential obstacles might arise, and how can I address them?**

   - Plan strategies to overcome anticipated challenges.

3. Monthly Reflection Prompts

Monthly Review Prompts

1. **What were the highlights of this month?**

   - Reflect on significant positive experiences to reinforce a sense of achievement.

2. **What did I learn about myself this month?**

   - Gain self-awareness by considering personal growth and insights.

3. **What were my biggest challenges, and how did I handle them?**

   - Analyze your responses to challenges to improve coping strategies.

4. **How have I progressed towards my long-term goals?**

   - Review your progress and adjust plans as needed to stay on track.

Mindfulness and Self-Care Prompts

1. **How often did I practice self-care this month?**

   - Assess the frequency and quality of your self-care activities.

2. **What activities helped me feel most centered and calm?**

   - Identify the most effective practices for maintaining mental clarity and reducing stress.

3. **What can I do next month to enhance my well-being?**

- Plan new self-care activities or improve existing routines.

4. **What am I most grateful for this month?**

- Reflect on gratitude to foster a positive mindset and emotional resilience.

4. Deep Reflection Prompts

Exploring Overthinking

1. **What situations typically trigger my overthinking?**

- Identify common triggers to understand and address the root causes of your overthinking.

2. **What thoughts tend to recur when I overthink?**

- Recognize recurring thought patterns to develop strategies for challenging them.

3. **How does overthinking affect my daily life?**

- Reflect on the impact of overthinking on your well-being and daily activities.

4. **What beliefs underlie my tendency to overthink?**

- Examine core beliefs that may contribute to overthinking and consider ways to shift them.

Developing New Perspectives

1. **How can I reframe my negative thoughts into positive ones?**

    - Practice cognitive restructuring by turning negative thoughts into constructive alternatives.

2. **What evidence do I have that contradicts my overthinking?**

    - Challenge your thoughts by seeking evidence that disproves them.

3. **What strengths can I draw on to manage my overthinking?**

    - Identify personal strengths that can help you cope with and reduce overthinking.

4. **How can I practice acceptance and let go of perfectionism?**

    - Develop strategies for embracing imperfection and reducing the pressure to be perfect.

Use these journaling prompts regularly to explore your thoughts, gain insights, and apply the techniques from "Think Clear: Simple Practices to Eliminate Overthinking." By making journaling a consistent practice, you can enhance your self-awareness, manage overthinking more effectively, and cultivate a clearer, more focused mind.

Appendix C: Online Resources and Apps

In today's digital age, numerous online resources and mobile applications can support you in your journey to reduce overthinking and improve mental clarity. This appendix provides a curated list of websites, online courses, and apps that offer tools, techniques, and support aligned with the practices discussed in "Think Clear: Simple Practices to Eliminate Overthinking."

1. Websites

1. Mindful.org

- **Description:** A comprehensive resource for mindfulness practices, offering articles, guided meditations, and courses to help you cultivate mindfulness in your daily life.

- **Website:** mindful.org

2. Anxiety and Depression Association of America (ADAA)

- **Description:** Provides resources and information on managing anxiety and depression, including tips on cognitive-behavioral techniques and stress management strategies.

- **Website:** adaa.org

3. Psychology Today

- **Description:** Features articles, blogs, and expert advice on a wide range of psychological topics, including overthinking, cognitive restructuring, and mental health.

- **Website:** psychologytoday.com

4. Verywell Mind

- **Description:** Offers accessible and evidence-based information on mental health topics, including tips and techniques for managing overthinking and improving emotional well-being.

- **Website:** verywellmind.com

5. Headspace

- **Description:** Provides articles and resources on mindfulness and meditation, including free guided meditations and techniques to reduce stress and overthinking.

- **Website:** headspace.com

2. Online Courses

1. Coursera: The Science of Well-Being

- **Description:** Offered by Yale University, this course explores the science behind happiness and well-being, teaching strategies to improve mental health and reduce overthinking.

- **Website:** coursera.org/learn/the-science-of-well-being

2. Udemy: Mindfulness Practitioner Course

- **Description:** A comprehensive course that covers mindfulness techniques, meditation practices, and strategies to manage stress and overthinking.

- **Website:** udemy.com/course/mindfulness-practitioner

3. Calm: Managing Stress and Anxiety

- **Description:** An online course focused on managing stress and anxiety through mindfulness and cognitive-behavioral techniques, provided by the Calm app.

- **Website:** calm.com

4. FutureLearn: Understanding Anxiety, Depression and CBT

- **Description:** A course that provides an introduction to cognitive-behavioral therapy (CBT) and its application in managing anxiety and overthinking.

- **Website:** futurelearn.com/courses/anxiety-depression-and-cbt

5. Mindful Schools: Mindfulness Fundamentals

- **Description:** An introductory course that teaches the fundamentals of mindfulness and how to incorporate mindfulness practices into daily life to reduce overthinking.

- **Website:** mindfulschools.org

3. Mobile Applications

1. Headspace

- **Description:** A leading app for mindfulness and meditation, offering guided meditations, sleep aids, and mindfulness exercises to help manage overthinking and stress.

- **Platforms:** iOS, Android

- **Website:** headspace.com

2. Calm

- **Description:** Provides guided meditations, sleep stories, breathing programs, and relaxing music to help reduce stress and overthinking.

- **Platforms:** iOS, Android

- **Website:** calm.com

3. Insight Timer

- **Description:** Features a vast library of free guided meditations, music tracks, and talks by mindfulness experts to help you practice mindfulness and reduce overthinking.

- **Platforms:** iOS, Android

- **Website:** insighttimer.com

4. CBT Thought Record Diary

- **Description:** A cognitive-behavioral therapy app that helps you track negative thoughts, challenge cognitive distortions, and develop healthier thinking patterns.

- **Platforms:** iOS, Android

- **Website:** cbtthoughtdiary.com

5. Stop, Breathe & Think

- **Description:** Offers personalized meditation and mindfulness exercises based on your current mood and needs, helping you to manage stress and overthinking.

- **Platforms:** iOS, Android

- **Website:** stopbreathethink.com

4. Support and Community Resources

1. 7 Cups

- **Description:** An online platform offering free, anonymous, and confidential text chat with trained listeners, as well as forums and self-help guides for managing stress and overthinking.

- **Website:** 7cups.com

2. Reddit: r/Mindfulness

- **Description:** A community forum for sharing experiences, tips, and resources related to mindfulness practice and reducing overthinking.

- **Website:** reddit.com/r/mindfulness

3. Anxiety and Depression Support Groups

- **Description:** A directory of online and in-person support groups for individuals dealing with anxiety and depression, providing community support and shared experiences.

- **Website:** adaa.org/supportgroups

4. The Mighty

- **Description:** An online community where people share their personal stories and insights on mental health, including overthinking and anxiety.

- **Website:** themighty.com

5. BetterHelp

- **Description:** An online counseling platform that connects you with licensed therapists for professional help in managing overthinking and other mental health issues.

- **Website:** betterhelp.com

These online resources and mobile applications are valuable tools to support your journey in managing overthinking and enhancing your mental clarity. Explore these options to find the ones that best suit your needs and preferences.

References

In the preparation of "Think Clear: Simple Practices to Eliminate Overthinking," a variety of sources have been consulted to ensure the information is accurate, current, and helpful. Below is a list of references that have contributed significantly to the content of this book. These sources include academic journals, books, reputable websites, and expert interviews, providing a solid foundation for the techniques and advice offered.

Books and Academic Texts

1. **Beck, Aaron T.** *Cognitive Therapy and the Emotional Disorders.* Meridian, 1979.

   - A seminal text on cognitive therapy that discusses how cognitive processes affect emotional disorders and provides foundational techniques for managing them.

2. **Kabat-Zinn, Jon.** *Full Catastrophe Living: Using the Wisdom of Your Body and Mind to Face Stress, Pain, and Illness.* Delta, 1990.

   - An introduction to mindfulness-based stress reduction (MBSR) and its applications in managing stress, pain, and illness through mindfulness techniques.

3. **Burns, David D.** *Feeling Good: The New Mood Therapy.* Harper, 1980.

   - A guide on cognitive-behavioral techniques that help individuals transform their thinking to improve their mood and reduce anxiety.

4. **Seligman, Martin E.P.** *Learned Optimism: How to Change Your Mind and Your Life.* Knopf, 1990.

   - Explores the concept of optimism and how changing pessimistic thought patterns can significantly impact mental health and resilience.

5. **Brown, Brené.** *The Gifts of Imperfection: Let Go of Who You Think You're Supposed to Be and Embrace Who You Are.* Hazelden Publishing, 2010.

   - Discusses the importance of embracing imperfection and vulnerability as sources of strength and authenticity.

Journal Articles

1. **Schwartz, Barry, and Sharpe, Kenneth E.** "Practical Wisdom: Aristotle Meets Positive Psychology," *Journal of Happiness Studies,* vol. 7, no. 3, 2006, pp. 377-395.

   - Investigates the intersection of classical philosophy and modern psychology in cultivating personal happiness and reducing overthinking.

2. **Hofmann, Stefan G., et al.** "The Efficacy of Cognitive Behavioral Therapy: A Review of Meta-analyses." *Cognitive Therapy and Research,* vol. 36, no. 5, 2012, pp. 427-440.

- A comprehensive review of the effectiveness of cognitive-behavioral therapy in treating various psychological disorders.

Websites and Online Resources

1. **American Psychological Association.** *APA PsycNet.*

- Provides a wealth of psychological research and resources, including studies on cognitive-behavioral techniques and mindfulness.

2. **National Institute of Mental Health.** *NIMH.*

- Offers information on mental health disorders, treatments, and tips for managing stress and mental health.

Conclusion

The references listed here form the backbone of the research and practical advice offered in "Think Clear: Simple Practices to Eliminate Overthinking." They are intended to provide readers with access to further reading and resources that can deepen their understanding and effectiveness in managing overthinking and improving mental health.